I0828654

SWARTHMORE COLLEGE.

DIMENSIONS.—Entire front, 348 feet; depth of center building, excluding kitchen, 110 feet; of the return wings, 92 feet.

AN

ESSAY ON EDUCATION

IN

THE SOCIETY OF FRIENDS.

BY

EDWARD PARRISH.

WITH AN

ACCOUNT OF THE PROCEEDINGS ON THE OCCASION OF LAYING THE CORNER-STONE OF SWARTHMORE COLLEGE.

'Tis education forms the common mind;
Just as the twig is bent the tree's inclined.
POPE.

PHILADELPHIA:
J. B. LIPPINCOTT & CO.
1866.

AN

ESSAY ON EDUCATION

IN

THE SOCIETY OF FRIENDS.

BY

EDWARD PARRISH.

WITH AN

ACCOUNT OF THE PROCEEDINGS ON THE OCCASION OF LAYING THE CORNER-STONE OF SWARTHMORE COLLEGE.

'Tis education forms the common mind;
Just as the twig is bent the tree's inclined.
POPE.

PHILADELPHIA:
J. B. LIPPINCOTT & CO.
1866.

EDUCATION

IN THE

SOCIETY OF FRIENDS.

INTRODUCTORY.

THIS essay is addressed to the members of the Religious Society of Friends, and to that numerous class who are descended from or affiliated with them.

A portion of it will be found especially applicable to those who, having inherited estates or prospered in business, have incurred the responsibilities attendant on the possession of means beyond their own needs.

Many such are free from the cares and expenses of a family, and hence naturally seek channels of beneficence into which to direct their surplus means. Others, having children, are sensible of the risks and responsibilities connected with their education, increased by the prospect of an estate sufficient to remove from them the necessity of active industry and thrift. Such are especially interested in providing facilities for guarded education, thus raising the standard of moral and intellectual culture in the community, while securing opportunities for their own immediate descendants.

The general extension of an elementary education among the masses is justly regarded as an essential element of the republican system. Its universal application has proved an inestimable boon to the Northern States—the absence of it, a prolific cause of evil in the South; and yet, is there not danger of our ideas being limited in regard to the education of our children by acquiescence in the comparatively low standard generally prevalent in the public schools?

Every one must feel that without that moral culture and restraint which home education is supposed to supply, the Common School, as provided by the State, falls far short of fitting the pupil for the duties of life, or even qualifying him as a good citizen; even in the matter of intellectual culture, these schools, as a class, fall far short of furnishing a good education.

The child is by nature absolutely ignorant of the laws of its physical, intellectual, and moral being and of the world into which it is born; and the extent to which it will acquire a full and complete development will be greatly dependent upon the bent given to its early aspirations and the advantages with which it is surrounded. In a few exceptional instances what men call genius gleams out from obscurity, and overcoming every obstacle asserts a pre-eminence which the world is brought to feel and acknowledge; but this is far from the ordinary history of the human mind.

It is by the stimulus of contact with active minds that the powers of the young are most obviously called forth, and, in general, in proportion to the talent and culture of those with whom it is early associated will be the progress of the forming and growing intellect.

The same remarks apply in a degree to the moral sense of children. Born negatively innocent, they sometimes display remarkable aptitude for appreciating and embracing truth. As in the one case genius may gleam forth with unexpected brilliancy from the least promising surroundings, so in the other the warmth of Divine love and the light of inspiration may be kindled in hearts least prepared by human culture. Yet the principle holds good, that the influence of the loving parent or teacher, full of affectionate counsel and admonition, and displaying daily and hourly fruits of righteousness and purity, is by far the strongest agency in promoting the moral and religious advancement of the young. Who cannot trace to such an influence much of the good existing in himself?

The simultaneous and complete development of the moral and intellectual nature of his offspring, not forgetting a due regard to physical culture, is the great object of every intelligent and conscientious parent, and as he looks to the means at his disposal to promote it, his thoughts most naturally turn to the Religious Society with which he is connected. It is indeed one of the highest and most important objects of religious organization to furnish those facilities for moral and intellectual improvement which are beyond the range of the family circle.

Friends have peculiarities, not of manners and forms only, but of principle, which are especially obvious in the moral training of their children. Without stating these in detail, it may serve our purpose to refer to a single feature in the faith of our Society, which all will recognize. It is that of the innate innocence of children, as contradistinguished from the dogma of original sin, as held by most orthodox churches.

This furnishes the key to that method of development which is beginning to be recognized by enlightened educators in and out of the Society,—the method which encourages and cultivates the best traits of character in the child, rather than attacks violently what may seem its unfavorable features of disposition. Caution, admonition, restraint, and even punishment, are occasionally necessary in dealing with the inexperienced and sometimes perverse, but to secure the affection and confidence of youth, to call into activity good motives and high aims, is by far the most easy and radical process of culture and development. It is a method peculiarly in accordance with the genius of Quakerism,—peculiarly favorable to the growth of that peaceable spirit which should distinguish the Society of Friends.

The sense of right and wrong present in the child from the early dawn of intelligence—the feeling which brings happiness for good and pain for wrong-doing—the swift witness—the light within—is pre-eminently recognized by Friends, and constitutes the basis of their moral teaching. If communicated to children in its simplicity, unincumbered by forms of expression which they cannot understand, it will answer to their experience, and furnish a means of moral training before which all external restraints and physical punishments fade into insignificance.

Strengthened by faith and enlightened by sound reason, this principle becomes a controlling influence through life, and the firm basis of a pure and indwelling piety.

The present tendency of reform in intellectual culture is peculiarly in harmony with the views of Friends. The question, "What knowledge is of most worth?" so ably answered in the recent popular essays of Herbert Spencer and others, was discussed forty years ago by Jonathan Dymond, a standard writer among Friends, whose "Essays on the Principles of Morality" should be in the hands of every student, and much the same conclusions were arrived at by him. Although in his days education, which had so long lain undisturbed on "the dregs of time," was the same as "before England had a literature of its own, and when Greek and Latin contained almost the sum of human knowledge," yet he forcibly advocated the idea that, "in general, science is preferable to literature,—the knowledge of things to the knowledge of words," and sketched a practical system of education adapted to the "middle ranks of society; that is, to the ranks in which the greatest sum of talent and virtue reside, and by which the business of the world is principally carried on."

There is doubtless some ultraism in the advocacy of modern schemes of educational reform; the ancient system of classical instruction must be admitted to have merits as a means of cultivating the memory and exercising the reasoning powers, which commend it to the favor of experienced teachers; but it is certainly out of the reach of the masses; and it seems to me the more liberal education is popularized, the more the classics must give way to the natural and physical sciences, which are calculated to furnish inexhaustible objects of profitable study and contemplation, besides being applicable to innumerable uses in practical life.

Nothing need be said in this connection in advocacy of liberal education for women.

Friends, of all sects, should be foremost, not only in throwing open the facilities at their command equally to both sexes, but in associating young men and girls in the lecture-room, the class-room, the lyceum, and, under proper supervision, in all appropriate plays and sports. It is fitting that they should grow up together in natural and mutually profitable intercourse, and ample experience shows that many of the evils of boarding-school and college life are thus materially lessened or entirely obviated.

It is not the purpose of this essay to appeal to any purely sectarian feeling—the matter in hand is of public and practical importance; but the author cannot ignore the force of those considerations which address themselves peculiarly to those connected with the Society of Friends.

To such as sincerely love and cherish the Society, and adhere intelligently to the spirituality of its faith and the simplicity of its forms, the object of the present essay cannot fail to commend itself; but there is a large class of nominal members and adherents of the Society, cherishing it through respect for its past history and its present high character, who yet feel little interest in its testimonies and little qualification for participating in its work. Such are invited to an examination of the subject of this essay. Its writer does not believe that the Society of Friends has outlived its usefulness, but, on the contrary, he maintains that in the matter of the education of youth, if in no other particular, it has an important sphere of usefulness and of duty.

More than two hundred years have passed since George Fox charged those who had been gathered chiefly through his ministry, to mind the light in their consciences. During most of this long period, those drawn into religious fellowship as Friends have exercised an influence for good which few of the present generation will gainsay. Mainly through their instrumentality the great doctrine that "God has come to teach his people himself," has been infused into religious teaching generally; through faithfulness to their enlightened convictions, liberty of conscience has been acknowledged, both in our own country and Great Britain, and powerful testimonies have been maintained against priestcraft and all oppression of the bodies and souls of men; against war with its barbarous and sinful concomitants; against intemperance, oaths, and many of the evils which afflict mankind. Both in Europe, where the organization of society at large was in direct antagonism to that Christian democracy which they preached, and in the Colonies of America, where their liberal institutions early developed a vigorous growth, these revivers of primitive Christianity gave a powerful impulse to enlightened and humane principles, the value of which is now recognized by many in all the Protestant sects.

It cannot be denied that this once powerful and united body, the representative of great and vital truths, has fallen a prey to the spirit of scism, and now exhibits the weakness which is an inevitable result. With a basis broad enough to take in every degree of Christian growth and experience, and an organization designed to secure perfect equality of rights among its members, it has not failed to illustrate the wickedness of intemperate zeal and proscriptive intolerance; the result, in great measure, of ignorance and prejudice —of a traditional rather than an intelligent appreciation of its principles. May we not hope that this last half of the nineteenth century will yet see the several fragments of the Society of Friends honestly burying past differences, rising above mere verbal standards of belief, and moving earnestly forward in the practical work of our day; each seeking its appropriate sphere of duty, and all willing to co-operate in the great labor of elevating the standard of morals and religion in the community?

THE PAST.

The Early Friends.

Notwithstanding the generally low state of education among the masses in England, at the period of the first rise of the Society of Friends, there are evidences that the early Friends generally were not deficient in respect for liberal learning, while there were many conspicuous instances among them of great literary and scholastic attainments.

It has been often remarked that the mission of George Fox, himself an illiterate man, was rendered more widely useful through the men of enlarged education who were among the early converts to his faith. This is doubtless equally true of the labors of those earnest and eloquent reformers by whom he was surrounded,—men who shook all England with their preaching, but many of whom have left to posterity no direct record of their views and opinions. It is mainly through Robert Barclay, Isaac Penington, and William Penn, all men of deep erudition, and each representing a somewhat different phase of religious opinion, that we are made acquainted with the principles and tenets of Friends in their day, and their works have even come to be regarded in our time in the light of standards of doctrine and practice.

Of these eminent characters, Robert Barclay was conspicuous for "great talents highly improved by education and seasoned by Divine grace;" and, although his life was cut short in his forty-second year, his services in establishing and strengthening the foundations of the sect to which he was an early convert, and the extensive research displayed in his works, and the great learning with which he elucidated his views of Christian doctrine, have gained him a high place in the history of the stirring times in which he lived.

Isaac Penington was distinguished from

childhood for remarkable piety and spirituality, and having been very early converted to Quakerism, became an eminent instrument in advancing the great work to which he was called. As an evidence of the educational condition of the circle in which he moved, the experience of Thomas Ellwood, who, when quite young, was intimate in his family, possesses considerable interest.

Deploring his own want of learning, through neglect of early opportunities, of which want he was not rightly sensible until he came among Friends, Thomas Ellwood says: "But I then both saw my loss and lamented it, and applied myself with the utmost diligence at all leisure times to recover it, so false I found that charge to be, which in these times was cast as a reproach upon the Quakers that they despised and derided all human learning." This was said "because they denied it to be essentially necessary to a Gospel Ministry, which was one of the controversies of the times."

Desiring to pursue his classical studies,

Thomas Ellwood, through his friend Isaac Penington, was introduced to the poet Milton, who, then wholly blind, received him at his apartments in London to read to him in such of the classics as he should appoint. After greatly improving himself, he became competent to instruct the children of Isaac Penington, by whom he was employed as tutor. He became one of the best writers among his contemporaries.

The biography of William Penn, which we have not space to dwell upon in this essay, should be studied, not only by every young man in the religious society in which he was an eminent member, and in the great Commonwealth he founded, but by all who would contemplate an example of unsullied purity of character combined with great talents, liberal education, and a sphere of usefulness such as has opened to few men in history.

In direct relation to our subject, a single paragraph may be quoted from his well-known letter to his wife in regard to the education of their children: "For their learning, be liberal, spare no cost, for by such parsimony all is lost that is saved; but let it be useful knowledge, such as is consistent with truth and godliness, not cherishing a vain conversation or idle mind, but ingenuity mixed with industry is good for the body and mind too."

English Schools.

As early as 1667, we find George Fox recommending the establishment of two boarding schools,—one for boys and one for girls; and in 1680, he mentions visiting them. At the boys' school, at Waltham Abbey, both ancient and modern languages were taught, as recommended during successive years by the London Yearly Meeting. Advice was further extended, "that young men of genius in low circumstances be furnished with means to procure requisite education; and in forming the character, the social animal being must not be overlooked, but the arts and sciences, which might fit him to perform his duties, better his condition, and supply his wants, must be included." The Shacklewell School for young men and girls, which was nearly contemporaneous, was established "for the teaching of whatsoever things were civil and useful in creation."

Somewhat in accordance with this is the design so quaintly expressed in the bequest by which George Fox conveyed to Friends the property at Fair Hill, Philadelphia, now associated with tender memories as the resting-place of many of our departed—"for a meeting-house and school-house and a burying-place, and for a play-ground for the children of the town to play on, and for a garden to plant with physical plants for lads and lasses to know simples and learn to make oils and ointments."

Among the earliest Friends' schools in England were the one at Gildersome, in Yorkshire, and "Friends' School-house and Workhouse," at Clerkenwell, an out-parish of the City of London, the latter supported almost entirely by Friends of London Quarterly

Meeting. This was connected with a kind of alms-house for the accommodation of Friends in necessitous circumstances, which is mentioned by the eminent Dr. John Fothergill, in a publication issued by him, as one of the reasons of its want of entire success.

It was in the London Yearly Meeting of 1778, that the establishment of one central school to meet the wants of the Society was determined upon, and the property was purchased at Ackworth, in Yorkshire, about one hundred and eighty miles from London, where the school still so widely known and valued was established. In 1779, Ackworth School was opened with seventy male and fifty-three female pupils; the number was afterward increased to near three hundred; and, according to the report for 1862, was in that year two hundred and ninety-six. Although the branches taught were originally only the English language, writing, and arithmetic, the grade of instruction has been gradually elevated to meet the demands of the times, and there can be no doubt that the influence of this institution has been of incalculable advantage, not only to individuals, but to the Society by which it has been fostered and endowed.

American Schools.

The founder of Pennsylvania, during the year after his arrival in his province, engaged the services of a teacher to open a school in Philadelphia, and in 1697 he founded the school, still in existence, though removed from its former well-known locality in Fourth Street below Chestnut, under care of "The Overseers of the Public School founded by Charter in the Town and County of Philadelphia, in Pennsylvania." In this school Latin and Greek and mathematics were early taught. Through a long course of years not a few of the eminent citizens of Philadelphia have in it realized the truth inscribed upon its corporate seal—"Good instruction is better than riches."

It has been often observed that the meeting-houses erected by our forefathers throughout the agricultural sections of Pennsylvania and New Jersey are connected, in many conspicuous instances, with ample school-houses, —monuments of the zeal of those pioneers in this new land to associate with the religious element in their polity suitable provision for intellectual training.

The example set by English Friends in the establishment and endowment of Ackworth School was soon followed in the infant States of America. A pamphlet by Owen Biddle, printed in Philadelphia in 1790, was specially devoted to the advocacy of a school, to be established "within the limits of the Yearly Meeting for Pennsylvania and New Jersey." Already a Friends' school of limited extent had been maintained at Nottingham, Chester County; but the views advocated in this publication were comprehensive, and with "a just sense of the importance of some such establishment," and of the ability of the Society to erect and maintain it, the author zealously bespeaks the aid of the wealthy in large donations, and of all, according to their means, to build up an institution which would be "extensively useful, attract the attention of the Society at large, and add a reputation to it."

A long and persistent labor was necessary to awaken the minds of Friends to the subject, and it was not until 1799 that West-Town Boarding School was opened. The history of this concern, as gathered from the unpublished correspondence* of those who carried it through, would occupy more space than comports with the scope of this essay; but the result accomplished is full of encouragement to those who would now seek to disturb the apathy and overcome the opposition toward an institution aiming at the improvement and elevation of thousands yet unborn.

During the sixty-six years which have elapsed since West-Town was opened, about five thousand one hundred and fifty girls and three thousand nine hundred and fifty boys

* Some of these letters, now in the hands of a Friend, are of considerable interest, and it is hoped they will at some future time be made public.

have participated in its advantages,—an aggregate of nine thousand members of the Society of Friends. Who can estimate its influence in furnishing the minds and forming the characters of these?

The history of the establishment of the "New England Yearly Meeting Boarding School" is closely connected with the biography of Moses Brown, of Providence, R. I., described by his contemporaries as "a judge, a counsellor, an elder, worthy of double honor." As early as 1780, it appears a subscription was opened, to which he was a liberal contributor, "for the establishment of a school for the more select and guarded education of Friends' children;" but the means of Friends being generally limited, and the sums subscribed mostly small, it was not until 1784 that the school was opened. After four years, it was discontinued on account of the inadequacy of its funds, and what remained of the principal was invested and increased by some additional contributions, until in 1814 Moses Brown offered to the Yearly Meeting forty-three acres of ground at Providence, since augmented by a bequest in his will of another lot of land near the premises; an additional effort being now made to increase the interest and active co-operation of Friends, the buildings were erected, and in 1819 the school was opened. Its venerable patron died in 1836, aged nearly a century, and the institution has grown and prospered, continuing to diffuse its benefits to large numbers to the present time, and its numerous alumni, at their annual meetings attest their love and gratitude to their Alma Mater.

Among those in former generations with whom the subject of the literary and religious education of children was one of life-long interest, was Joseph Tallcot, of Dutchess County, New York, who, while at times engaged as a teacher from a sense of duty, was a zealous advocate of associated action to extend the blessings of education among Friends generally. From Nine Partners' Preparative Meeting, of which he was a member, a proposition went up, through the regular channels, to the Yearly Meeting of New York, in 1794, as a result of which the Nine Partners' Boarding School was opened in 1797: it was soon filled with children from various parts of New York, and from a few places more remote. The reminiscences of this institution as related by some of its early pupils, still living, while they exhibit in a striking manner the vast improvements in literary and scientific education during sixty years, show the happy results of the religious care and concern of those having Friends' schools in charge in those primitive times.

"Fairhill Boarding School," established by subscription about the year 1820, by Baltimore Yearly Meeting, was in successful operation as a "Yearly Meeting School" about ten years; it has been, of late, in private hands, somewhat under the auspices of the Society.

With these brief notices, we conclude the sketch of the more ancient Friends' schools, and come down to our own times, in search of evidences of zeal for the culture and advancement of the young.

THE PRESENT.

TURNING from the efforts of our forefathers to surround their children with educational advantages, we are compelled, at the outset, to acknowledge that the rapid strides which have been made by the community at large have left the Society of Friends, as a whole, far in the background.

Since the unhappy division in 1827, which has been characterized by a leading statesman of Pennsylvania as "the greatest misfortune which ever happened to the City of Philadelphia," that portion of the Society which embraces much the largest number of members within the limits of Philadelphia, New York, and Baltimore Yearly Meetings, has not a single institution calculated to centralize the learning and science of the Society, and to foster and encourage liberal education —not one in which our children can obtain the advantages of a really liberal education under circumstances favorable to their becoming attached to the religious organization of which they are members.

The inquiry as to what Friends' schools within the reach of our members are best adapted to impart a liberal education, brings into view several of the ancient seats of learning already referred to; these, with several others established in our time, may be mentioned under the following head:

Schools of Orthodox Friends.

The doors of "West-Town" are closed, on purely technical grounds, against many of those who are sincerely desirous to acquit themselves worthily as Friends, and whose ancestors contributed largely to its establishment and endowment, entitling them, in equity, to its benefits.

"Friends' Yearly Meeting School" at Providence, R. I., is not so restricted, and continues to receive some of the Friends' children excluded from West-Town; though remote from the largest settlements of Friends, it is worthy the attention of parents who desire to place their children, of either sex, under sound instructions in a healthful and pleasant location.

"Friends' Academy," at Union Springs, Cayuga County, N. Y., established in 1858, chiefly through the energy of John J. Thomas, of that place, and since taken in charge by the New York Yearly Meeting of Orthodox Friends, is a young and growing institution, open to all who are willing to conform to its rules.

"The Howland Institute," of the same place, is confined to young women and girls; it is yet in its infancy, but, from the liberality displayed in its endowment and the excellent auspices under which it has been commenced, we may anticipate for it a career of extended usefulness in the future.

For some years past a limited number of our young men have resorted to Haverford College, which, though originally established as a "select school," was found to require support from outside the pale of that part of the Society by whose members it was erected. This institution is a monument to the zeal and liberality of its founders, and, during near thirty years in which it has been in operation, has sent forth many young men of solid classical and mathematical attainments. It is, however, too expensive an institution, and too limited in its scope, to meet the views of the great mass of Friends, besides being confined only to one sex.

Earlham College, located at Richmond, Indiana, is another and more recent evidence of the enterprise of that portion of the Society, which, perhaps partly from retaining its connection with English Friends, and enjoying their counsel and assistance,* has sought to bring some, among the generations to come, under friendly influences, while imparting to them the blessings of liberal learning.

---

* Joseph John Gurney, during his tour in the Western States, aided the establishment of this institution, which bears the name of his estate in England, by a liberal donation.

Though controversies have embittered the past, and different forms of expression, and even different modes of faith, which have existed in the Society from its rise, have, through the divergence caused by the spirit of controversy, put barriers between those once united as Friends, surely all can rejoice when the zeal of the Society takes a practical direction toward the development of the intellectual powers, and the consequent diffusion of more enlarged and liberal views among those who are to come after us.

Private Boarding and Neighborhood Schools.

In this review of educational advantages —past and present—we must not overlook the private boarding schools kept by Friends, some of which have a high reputation far beyond the limits of the Society, or the day schools under the care of Monthly Meetings, of which those in the Cities of New York, Philadelphia, Baltimore, Wilmington, Del., West Chester, Pa., and a few other places, are especially worthy of mention.

The policy of confining these schools to members of the Society has generally, of latter years, been superseded by that of excluding no pupils of good character who are willing to conform to the rules. While this, without due care, may produce overcrowding in Friends' schools, it has the advantage of securing larger remuneration to the teachers and improved facilities for instruction; the benefits are also diffused and good feeling promoted on the part of those of other denominations. It has been found, under this liberal policy, that Friends' schools, when well conducted, overflow with pupils, notwithstanding there are plenty of free schools near at hand.

The eminent success of these day schools in the cities is cause of encouragement to the Society to improve and extend the educational advantages furnished in smaller towns and in agricultural districts,—to secure the very best of teachers, and to pay these well in view of the onerous duties of their calling, the high moral and intellectual qualities it requires, and the responsibilities it imposes.

Viewed with reference to the opportunities they afford for moral and religious instruction, and to their possible influence in perpetuating and extending the Society, these schools can hardly be overestimated. The spectacle of so large a number of intelligent and bright countenances as are assembled from these schools at meetings for worship, has been the occasion for many fitting words of counsel from Friends in the ministry, and has frequently been remarked upon as most inspiring to such as are advancing in life, and naturally look with emotion upon those who in their turn must follow them.

Culture of the Soil versus Mental Culture.

It is deplorable that many in the agricultural communities which constitute so large a portion of the membership of the Society of Friends in America, evince quite as much interest in the cultivation of the soil, and in realizing its products, as in the development of the minds of their children.

Such are satisfied with the elementary schools maintained at public expense, none of which reach a high ideal of school education. In these the children are often thrown into unprofitable associations without any adequate advantages in the way of intellectual training. The public school system, in the establishment of which Friends had so large a share, is, undoubtedly, to the State at large, an inestimable blessing: yet it has had a tendency to satisfy many people in good circumstances with comparatively careless and inadequate instruction, and to lessen the zeal formerly felt among Friends to be in advance of the community in the moral and intellectual grade of their schools.

Of the large number of "Monthly Meeting Schools,"* mostly established at much sacrifice by Friends of former generations, some of them so endowed as to be free of expense, or nearly so, to members of the Society, many

* Of these there were in Philadelphia Yearly Meeting, in 1864, forty-three, thirty-seven of which are taught by members of the Society—1867 children were comprised in these.

suffer from want of intelligence and active interest on the part of committees to whom they are intrusted; it is a common complaint that the teachers employed are frequently inadequately paid and lack the qualifications to make the schools efficient. The capacities of the pupils are thus but poorly developed from lack of that stimulus which a thorough and pervading interest in intellectual advancement can alone bring into action.

Thus it happens that a large proportion of the talent of the Society lies undeveloped, the few whose minds have been awakened to the contemplation of the facts of science,—who have been brought into converse with the great intellects who have explored the secrets of the universe, find but little interest in such ennobling pursuits among the great mass of their Friends. Some of these constantly regret that the circumstances of their early life were unfavorable to the awaking of their intellectual powers, while others are even too ignorant to value the advantages they have failed to realize, and busy themselves in decrying that which they do not appreciate, because they cannot understand.

The history of the Society shows that there have always been some among its members who, in their opposition to an educated class, such as the clergy in other denominations, have ceased to value learning properly as the right of all, failing to see that the absence of a distinct profession, embodying the learning of the Society and monopolizing the power which learning brings, should constitute a strong motive for the general diffusion of knowledge and the multiplication of facilities for imparting it. As each individual undoubtedly has some place to occupy in the Society, and in the community at large, there should be, it would seem, such a system of development that each should find his place and be qualified to fill it.

How widely different from this is the actual state of things! We sometimes find the farmer wedded to his land, fearing lest some of his sons may perhaps seek other employment—lest, if educated beyond the supposed requirements of a manual occupation, they may leave it and be found among the haunts of men, busy with affairs which call forth their faculties and exercise the talents which the all-wise Creator has implanted in them.

It is mournful to see, in the thriving agricultural communities of Friends, how the services of the whole family are often taxed to the utmost upon the drudgery of the farm—how the lad of sixteen, each winter enjoys but a few months' schooling in the neighborhood school; his sister, a talented young woman, perhaps the future mother of a family of immortal beings, who are to draw from her their first ideas of truth and duty and take the mould of their mental characters from her own, is found laboring early and late in the dairy and household, cumbered with cares which should come only with mature years, and debarred from the glorious light of knowledge which can alone expand her faculties and fit her for the exalted position to which she is called.

In these strictures no invidious distinction is intended between persons devoted to agriculture and those engaged in mechanical and commercial pursuits. It is believed that there are those among all classes who fail to appreciate the undoubted right of their children, not only to the knowledge for which they so often crave, but also to opportunities calculated to create desires for improvement, and to foster high and worthy aims.

It is the experience of some that "necessity knows no law," but where there is abundance of the good things of this life there is no excuse for neglecting the full development of the faculties of our children. In no branch of domestic expenditure is parsimony so misplaced, in nothing is it so inexcusable as in the matter of education—better that the children should grow up without a dollar to begin life with, than that they should come to manhood and womanhood without their faculties being awakened and their intellects expanded by liberal learning.

Cause and Effect.

Viewed in its relations to the perpetuity of the Society of Friends and the spread of its principles, indifference to the subject of education may be regarded both as an effect and a cause—an effect of lukewarmness in regard to religious duties, and as a propagating cause of the same evil.

In strong contrast to the zeal of our early predecessors in contending for their principles in the midst of persecution and even death, we find the Society now quietly resting in its traditions and forms, its members generally illustrating in private life the virtues which have grown out of its discipline and teaching, but almost devoid of that *animus* which made their early predecessors a great power in the earth. Toleration, secured by the faithfulness of our forefathers, finds most of us at ease in the pursuit of our private interests, but little concerned to maintain our organization, and almost tempted to chime in with the sentiment of those modern writers who have maintained that the usefulness and the influence of the Society are at an end.

Too many of our children are brought up in ignorance of the instructive history of the Society, and of its instrumentality in promoting human rights and spreading practical views of Christianity; they are strangers to the examples presented in the biography of the great and good men who have illustrated its principles and borne its testimonies before the world, and they fail from lack of instruction, to appreciate those principles and testimonies, and to gain that thorough acquaintance with their meaning and scope which can alone make them efficient instruments in their maintenance and diffusion.

Do we not here recognize a leading cause of the weakness which concerned members of the Society mourn? As this is a direct effect of unwarrantable indifference to one of the most obvious duties incumbent on individuals and religious organizations, is it not also an obvious cause of increasing declension and weakness?

Five Years' Review.

Those who appreciate the state of facts exhibited in the foregoing pages, and desire the welfare of the children of our own and succeeding generations, will be prepared to rejoice that measures are now in progress to provide an institution adapted to the educational wants of the Society of Friends.

In the autumn of 1860, a company collected socially at the house of a much esteemed Friend in Baltimore, became interested in conversing upon the state of education, and a desire was expressed that means should be adopted which would lead to a higher appreciation of scientific and classical learning and its more general diffusion throughout the Society. Accordingly on the second of Tenth Month, 1860, a meeting was convened, at which the venerable Benjamin Hallowell, a veteran teacher, presented the plan which had lain many years near his heart of establishing a school, under the care of Friends, at which an education may be obtained equal to that of the best institutions of learning in our country, and adapted especially to qualify Friends of both sexes for the charge of family and neighborhood schools heretofore languishing for lack of efficiency in their teachers.

The idea entered into this concern of elevating, as well the moral as the intellectual standard of education, and of promoting the growth and influence of the Society of Friends, beginning where such labor can alone be effectual with the young, the receptive, growing, and expanding. Such a design could not fail to be appreciated by those to whom it was explained, and a committee was chosen to prepare an address setting forth the objects in view, and to solicit the co-operation of the larger bodies of Friends in Philadelphia and New York.

An address was prepared forthwith, and read at Conferences, held in Philadelphia on the 28th of Eleventh Month, and in New York on the 10th of Twelfth Month following. Committees were appointed at each of these to co-operate with Baltimore Friends in the prosecution of the concern. It is yet too soon to write the history of this most important movement, but if the measures then inaugurated should be crowned with the promised success, the names of those who were thus foremost in it will go down to posterity as worthy of double honor.

The printing and distribution of this address was so soon followed by those startling events which shook the nation to its center and have but recently culminated, that the efforts toward enlisting the great body of Friends, on behalf of this undertaking, may be said to have been inaugurated during the most anxious time of the great rebellion.

When many citizens doubted if they or their posterity would again enjoy the blessings of free government—when men of wealth held their possessions by so feeble a tenure that soon they might not command enough of this world's goods to feed and clothe their families—when parents, not a few, trembled lest their sons, swept into the current that carried so many thousands to untimely graves, would never return to comfort their declining years—when darkness, discouragement, and uncertainty hung over everything in the future, it seemed, to some, out of place to be planning great improvements or seeking to found beneficent institutions.

It was in the darkest hour that a voice was raised in our councils, which had many times before been heard in the midst of discouragements and even obloquy in defense of progress and principle,—the voice of one who had herself realized in early life the value of a Friends' school,—showing the pressing importance of those educational interests which must influence the welfare of society in any event and under all circumstances. So fully were these views realized, that it was resolved to persevere, presenting the subject in every community of Friends, where there was an ear to hear, and invoking the moral support and pecuniary aid of all.

Conferences were appointed in Friends' meeting-houses in city and country; sometimes these were largely attended; the subject was earnestly presented and subscriptions solicited in aid of the undertaking. A committee for promoting subscriptions to the fund met monthly at Race Street Meeting-house, Philadelphia, generally attended by some from the country; thus the interest was kept alive and the subscription extended.

The preliminary organization, under the name of Friends' Educational Association, passed through some difficulties in forming a constitution; unavoidable differences of sentiment upon technical points alienated a few whose influence has since been missed, but, to use the peculiar term so familiar to Friends, *the concern* continued to grow and increase.

At the Annual Meeting in Twelfth Month, 1862, fifty thousand dollars were reported as having been subscribed,—a sum which has since been nearly doubled. A Board of Managers was selected, consisting of Friends of both sexes from various sections of Pennsylvania, New Jersey, New York, and Maryland. This Board, which has been continued with little alteration, has moved in great harmony in the several measures rendered necessary by the progress of the movement, and when questions have arisen prematurely, the ground of confidence has been maintained, not only by the officers toward each other, but by the great body of subscribers toward the Board. The selection of a location for the proposed institution called forth a zealous advocacy of different sites, and was followed by corresponding disappointment among those whose advocacy was unsuccessful, but the expression by vote of a large majority of the stock, as provided by the constitution, was a final settlement of the question.

In the course of this work, members of the Board, and others interested, have attended conferences in nearly all the Monthly Meetings within the compass of Philadelphia Yearly Meeting, numbering fifty, obtaining subscriptions from Friends; besides addressing conferences in several sections of New

5

York and Baltimore Yearly Meetings, and one at Farmington, within the limits of Genesee Yearly Meeting.

In all these they have found some to respond cordially to their appeals. The young, who, in many sections in the midst of indifference and apathy are impatiently thirsting for knowledge; parents who begin to appreciate the imperative duty they owe to their rising families, to supply them with the highest possible culture and development; and lastly, the elders and fathers in the church, who in looking for a succession of standard-bearers, begin to suspect that to the neglect of the great interests of education under the guarded care of the Society, may be attributed much of the weakness which they deplore.

PROSPECTIVE.

Swarthmore College.

It is proposed, under this head, to present to the reader a succinct account of the present condition, the objects, and plans of the corporation which has grown out of the Friends' Educational Association. In accordance with the original design, to furnish a complete course of study in the higher branches of knowledge, especially with a view to qualify teachers, it was early determined to give to the proposed institution the full grade of a college, under an act of incorporation from the State of Pennsylvania.

While this does not preclude an Academical Department, a Normal School, and a Model School, all of which are included in the plan, it requires the managers to supply instruction in the higher branches of knowledge which are not thoroughly taught in ordinary private institutions.

By means of the act of incorporation the

title to the property is defined and secured to those who contribute to purchase and build it; and in case of future controversies, it cannot be unfairly diverted from them. The name *Swarthmore College* is derived from the home of George Fox, after his marriage to Margaret Fell. At Swarthmore, near Ulverstone, in England, he himself owned a plot of ground, on which he erected a meeting-house, which is still standing.

The stockholders are not necessarily members of the Society of Friends,—a very considerable number of our fellow-citizens, and several in membership and by profession connected with the orthodox division of the Society, have, without solicitation, testified their interest in the spread of education by subscribing to the stock. The managers, however, are restricted by the charter to members of the Society of Friends; they are to be elected at the Annual Meeting, each stockholder having one vote. In all questions affecting the disposition of the property of the corporation, a stock vote is provided for.

The Site.

The property procured for the location of Swarthmore College is composed of a portion of that known as West-Dale, from having been the birth-place of Benjamin West, with contiguous land; it is located in Delaware County, Pennsylvania, about ten miles from Philadelphia, with which city it connects by the West Chester and Philadelphia Railroad, passing through the place, and furnishing a station at a convenient distance from the building site. It contains ninety-four acres and five perches of land, and is bounded on one side by the Springfield and Chester road, and on the other by Crum Creek, a winding and rapid stream. After a thorough examination of the rural districts surrounding Philadelphia, the managers were generally agreed that a more eligible location for such a purpose could scarcely be found. The land is high, commanding an extensive prospect of variegated scenery, and a distant view of the Delaware River, the ancient town of Chester, the first landing-place of William Penn in his Province, and Media, the county town, distant one and a half miles, in which, it may be remarked, the sale of liquor is prohibited by law, in all time to come. There are several springs contiguous to each other on the high ground, sufficient to furnish an abundant supply of pure water, and water-power to pump it to the required elevation. On the northwest the land is covered with an abundant growth of trees, adapted to afford protection to the grounds in winter; the wood-land is ample for shaded walks, and the banks of the stream afford a feature of romantic beauty rarely surpassed. The property cost $21,446.96.

The Building.

The Managers are not insensible to the mistake which has so often been made in carrying out such undertakings, of regarding the building as the paramount feature of the institution; in all their plans utility has been considered before elegance, and economy has constituted a leading motive. On the other hand, however, so much depends upon the convenient arrangement of a large establishment in securing its economical management, and so important is it to provide in the proposed institution for a large number of the several classes it is intended to accommodate, that a commodious building, capable of still further extension, seems quite necessary.

The original idea of separate buildings, in which something like the family relation might be maintained among the inmates, was found to require an outlay much beyond the cost of a single structure appropriately divided. The necessity of connecting corridors and adequate means of conveyance for the supplies when cooked, and other requirements of this plan, determined its abandonment and the union of its desirable features, as far as practicable, in a single stone structure.

This, as far as the plans have been matured, will consist of a center College building, containing dining-rooms, kitchen, lecture-room, library, reception-room, office, and dwelling for the resident officer; two wings parallel to this, each containing the residence of a teacher and his family, and dormitories for about fifty pupils, and, between these and the center building, connecting wings, containing class-rooms and dormitories, each wing accommodating about fifty pupils. The dormitories will be in size about 10 by 15 feet, designed to accommodate two single beds. The building thus projected will contain about one hundred and ten pupils of each sex, all under appropriate supervision, virtually separated in different houses, but so readily communicating with the central College building as that all may resort there to meals, to the morning and evening collections, to lectures, and for other purposes, without exposure to the weather.

Especial attention will be given to the ventilation, heating, and lighting of the establishment, and to provision against danger from fire; the stairways will be ample and partly fire-proof, and the isolation of each division will be such that it is hardly possible a fire could become general.

As it is designed to accommodate at least four hundred pupils, when the buildings are completed, the center building is planned with reference to that number, and additions are projected which will not interfere with the symmetry of the structure. An advantage anticipated from providing for so large a number of pupils is, that instruction can be proportionably cheapened as the number is extended. From all that can be learned in advance, and, from the estimate of an experienced teacher now engaged in a similar institution, it is believed that there will be enough to occupy all the accommodations provided, as soon as they are ready.

Several Departments.

It is proposed to include in Swarthmore College—*First.* An academical or preliminary department. *Second.* A normal department, with model school. *Third.* A collegiate department.

The Academical department is regarded as of least necessity, as the demand for common school education is already partly supplied by neighborhood schools, and by private boarding schools, which it is no part of the plan of this institution to supersede; and yet it is intended that this department shall be the first to be opened as a necessary preparation for the Collegiate. As private schools adapt their teaching to prepare pupils for the Collegiate department, this may have less importance in the general scheme of instruction; yet the experience of other institutions would indicate that a much larger number of pupils will avail themselves of the academical than of the full Collegiate course.

The Normal department will probably be a leading feature as soon as established; the demand for teachers, already everywhere apparent, must greatly increase, as the vast Southern country is opened to their labors; moreover, the spread of educational reform is bringing about a higher appreciation of the profession of teaching, and must call for

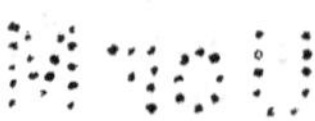

a better class, both of talents and attainments, in this, which Anthony Benezet justly characterized as "the most exalted duty a Christian mind can be engaged in."

Teaching has only recently been studied as a science; yet the normal school begins to be regarded as essential to the teacher for the same reason as a medical school is to the physician. He who would guide the child needs to be acquainted not only with the knowledge to be imparted, but how to impart it. He should make the faculties of the mind his study, and should know how to read not only the capacity of his pupil, but those secret springs—the affections, the passions, and ruling desires—which supply the motive-power to the intellect and give direction to the forming character.

For the exercise of the more advanced pupils in normal schools in the practice of teaching, model schools are maintained. These usually consist of classes engaged in acquiring the rudiments of learning, whose tuition is furnished them gratuitously, or at a moderate cost. By the establishment of such a department, a certain number of orphan children and others whose circumstances render it necessary that they should be placed from home when quite young, may be economically educated up to the point of entering the academical department. How far it may accord with the future policy of Swarthmore College to extend this department, will depend upon circumstances. May it not happen that some benevolently-disposed Friend will, out of his abundance, provide a home upon the delightful grounds of this College for a suitable number of orphans,—so generally recognized as objects of Christian charity,—thus promoting, at the same time, the efficiency of the Normal department?

The Collegiate department may be admirably connected with the Normal—the branches taught, with the exception of the theory and practice of teaching, which might or might not be included in the College curriculum, may be the same in both, though it would not, perhaps, be required of all graduates in the Normal, to go through the complete course in the Collegiate. Experience and a mature consideration of the subject, by those engaged as professors and teachers, when the institution is organized, will doubtless develop a policy which cannot now be foreshadowed. It is, however, to be desired that all students who carry from this college its diploma, will have learned so much of the art of teaching as to make them more useful in communicating the knowledge they have acquired than is the case with young men generally, who graduate at our colleges. "To do good and communicate" should ever be the pleasure, as it is duty, of those who have enjoyed the advantages of a liberal education.

The peculiar advantage of such a course as a well-directed Normal School would furnish to young women, is obvious from the fact that the large majority of these are destined to rear children, and, in the exercise of this highest duty, the knowledge of how to teach removes them in a degree from the necessity of sending away their offspring at a tender age to be trained by others who, whatever qualifications they may possess, cannot be animated by the tenderness and earnestness of a mother,—the guardian and teacher appointed by Providence, in the order of nature, to rear the coming generation.

Relation of the Sexes at School.

It is confidently believed that the experience of Swarthmore College will be similar to that of other institutions in which young men and young women, at the age in which they are pursuing the higher branches of knowledge, are advantageously associated in the lecture-room, the class-room, the lyceum, at the table, and, with proper restrictions, in the ordinary sports appropriate to college life. The impression, with some, that such association would distract the mind from a due attention to study, and lead to the frivolity so deplored in ordinary society, is not justified by the facts. The mental attrition of the class-room is especially favorable to students forming a just estimate of each other's capacity, and thus losing false ideas of perfection in each other, the frequent source of romantic attachments. Constantly subjected to artless association and competition, they seldom exhibit that unnatural constraint and coyness which distinguish the unaccustomed intercourse of boys and girls, when first thrown together in what is called society; while, under the constant supervision of teachers, any exceptional instances of undue intimacy soon become the subject of observation, and it may be, of suitable admonition and interference.

The Scheme of Instruction.

It would be premature to sketch a plan of instruction in the present stage of this enterprise, and it is only in answer to repeated inquiries that I shall venture to state the views of the managers as far as they have been matured and found expression. It is proposed to give greater prominence to the physical, natural, and chemical sciences than is common in ordinary colleges. Science is the key that unlocks the world we live in, and unfolds to us the philosophy of our daily pursuits. Our food, our clothing, our houses, the methods of warming and ventilating, the drainage and improvement of the land, the cultivation of crops, the preservation of health of ourselves and of the animals under our care—are all legitimate scientific studies, ministering to our comfort through life, and guarding us against many popular errors founded in ignorance and superstition. It is, moreover, a direct result of scientific studies to enlarge our conception of the wisdom and goodness of the Creator, and to furnish innumerable and instructive parallels from the external universe illustrative of those sublime spiritual truths, which are so admirably conveyed to the mind by comparison with objects which are visible and tangible.

Oral and experimental instruction are especially aimed at in this connection. Nothing so fastens the attention and impresses the memory as a direct demonstration of a great truth by experiment. Every lecturer must have observed how the most sluggish student, who will fall asleep over books, and even wander from a subject eloquently and cogently presented in words, will instantly seize upon an experimental illustration, and often comprehend it more fully than others who might be considered far more appreciative. Hence the importance of ample apparatus for illustrating the facts of chemical and physical science, which are opening to philosophers, in our day, richer fields for discovery than any heretofore presented in the history of science. With a view, also, to thorough acquaintance with practical chemistry, it is designed to establish a laboratory in which the chemical class can be carried through a course of analysis.

Natural history is also proposed to be taught, and an extensive cabinet aimed at, illustrative of every department of this study. It is a subject of profound regret to many thinkers in our country, that there is so little for the people to see of the works of creation, classified scientifically, and giving an idea of the gradations by which every created thing is linked into—

> " . . . . . . One stupendous whole,
> Whose body Nature is, and God the soul."

The beautiful grounds belonging to the College will, it is hoped, be planted with a great variety of trees, furnishing a study of practical interest to those especially who are so favored as to enjoy future opportunities for country life. A garden of classified plants would be quite practicable, and would be a rare attraction in our country, besides furnishing to the pupils an opportunity to become practical botanists with a facility enjoyed by none of their predecessors. It may be thought that the managers are laying out plans which none of them will probably live to execute, but this should not discourage them from working "while it is called day," trusting that others may enter into their labors, and that so desirable a consummation may be realized by those who may come after them.

It is not deemed necessary to speak at large of the higher mathematics, the ground-work of so much that is practical in science, and a means of mental discipline universally regarded as in the highest degree important. Nor of language, which, viewed as a science, is one of the most profound that can claim the attention of the human intellect. There are capacities and tastes especially suited to this study, and, as a means of disciplining the mind, exercising the memory, and forming the judgment, it is a necessary element in our scheme of education; besides, the practical application of Latin and Greek to the nomenclature of the sciences, and to a thorough understanding of our own and the other modern languages, makes an acquaintance with them essential to a thorough student,—especially to one who is to teach others.

History, intellectual philosophy, the principles of morality, as maintained by Friends, which are confidently believed to be far in advance of those ordinarily taught, will all be subjects to be introduced into the course of instruction at Swarthmore College, as its means increase, and the properly qualified teachers are found. A caution rests on the minds of the members of the Board to introduce no unprofitable subjects of controversy into this institution; and it is their firm belief that as solid and substantial learning is imparted upon subjects of practical interest, less importance will be attached to visionary ideas, and less interest felt in useless speculations.

Systems of education are now somewhat in a transition state. Allusion has been made in the Introduction to this essay to views which have obtained among enlightened Friends in the past, and which are advocated by numerous writers in our time, looking toward the introduction of the practical element more prominently into advanced systems of education. Our Government has acted upon this idea in appropriating a large amount of the public domain to the maintenance of schools in which theoretical and practical science must be leading features. The testing of the capacity of these to develop a high intellectual culture fitted to the conditions and requirements of American life, is peculiarly a work of our day. In parting with the aristocratic idea of an educated class, should we not adopt the democratic idea of an education open to all who have the talent to avail themselves of it and adapted to prepare men and women for the higher walks in agriculture, the mechanic arts, trade, and business of every kind, as well as for what have been termed the learned professions?

Far be it from me to restrict the idea of an education to mere preparation for business; no scheme of teaching deserves that name which does not aim to prepare the pupil for mental employments beyond the range of practical life, to open channels of profitable reflection and study leading to pure and rational enjoyment, embellishing and refining the whole character and the life. Such an education should be kept in view by every parent who would qualify his children for active usefulness and rational enjoyment, and such, it is confidently believed, will be aimed at by those intrusted with framing the future policy and superintending the management of Swarthmore College.

Financial.

Various estimates have been made of the cost of the required college buildings, but the uncertainty in regard to the price of material and labor makes it impossible to determine this in advance. With a view to avail ourselves of the anticipated decline in prices, the contracts will, for the present, include only portions of the building at a time, the digging of cellars and laying foundations during the present autumn, the erection of a portion of the walls above ground in the spring, and so forth, the intention being to build such parts first as will avail for the purposes of the Academical department. In no event are all the buildings likely to cost less than $200,000, and their furniture and apparatus $50,000. Of this aggregate, about $70,000 is now in hand.

There will be pressing necessity to push the subscriptions vigorously to enable the work to go on to speedy completion, but we are encouraged by the experience of similar institutions to believe that when built, Swarthmore College will be a nucleus around which much of the benevolence and public spirit of the Society will gather,—that future donations and bequests will enable the managers to enlarge the facilities for instruction at the same time that they lower its cost and extend its blessings to many who would otherwise be deprived of it from want of means.

We necessarily postpone to the future the opening of subscriptions toward the establishment of scholarships, giving education and subsistence to meritorious pupils; toward the creation and augmentation of an ample library, to which valuable contributions of books have already been promised; toward the collection of a museum of natural history and art, and the purchase of astronomical apparatus, none of which are included in our present estimates. Our aim is to *build and open this College* with the *necessary* means of instruction *as soon as possible.*

We cannot doubt the abundant means in the Society of Friends to erect and maintain any institution which the interests of their children or of the Society demand. There is wealth enough. Some individual members could erect and endow this college without abridging a single comfort of life, and there are many who could well afford subscriptions of such amounts as rapidly to make up the fund required; and it may be safely stated of Friends generally, that there are few who could not afford to take one or more shares in the stock. Add to this the assistance proffered by some not in membership, who desire an opportunity of aiding in the good work, and anticipate sharing its advantages, and we have every reason to expect that success will attend the effort.

Friends have fewer calls upon their liberality in connection with the support of their religious institutions than others; they have no clergy to support—no missionary enterprises

—their meeting-houses are plain, and require little expenditure—their habits, as individuals, are generally economical—their industry and thrift almost proverbial, so that they rarely fail to accumulate property. It is, indeed, in this habit of accumulation that one of their chief snares lies hidden; "habit is second nature," and it is often hard to unlearn in later life what in youth was properly held up as a virtue—the habit of saving. On the other hand, no one who has not accustomed himself to it knows the luxury of giving, and especially of seeing the fruits of his bounty.

The uselessness of money to its possessor, except to the extent of providing comforts and means of rational enjoyment, and its immense value when appropriated toward the advancement and happiness of others, are only fully apparent to such as have learned how to administer their own estates for objects of real utility and beneficence. May it not be said with truth, that only such realize the fullest enjoyment from wealth, or find it promotive of their highest interests?

It is a common observation that many men of large means have left estates to purposes of public utility, whose benevolent intentions have been inadequately carried out by those intrusted with the disposal of their bequests; and it seems to be a growing determination of the benevolent to give, during their lifetime, toward such objects as present themselves in the light of public benefactions, discriminating according to their own judgment, and themselves sharing in the pleasurable occupation of appropriating their means.

The munificent donation of Matthew Vassar for the establishment of a Female College at Poughkeepsie, New York, already amounting to several hundred thousands of dollars—the recent offer of Ezra Cornell, of Ithaca, New York, of half a million dollars and about 200 acres of land, for the establishment, with the aid of funds appropriated to the State by the U. S. Government, of a college to provide instruction in such branches of learning as are related to agriculture and the mechanical arts; and the still more recent offer of a like sum, by Asa Packer, a wealthy citizen of Pennsylvania, toward a college to be located in this State, all show an appreciation of the value of education, and offer noble examples to those who, as stewards over abundance of this world's goods, must feel the responsibility of giving an account of their stewardships.

While these considerations are respectfully offered to the wealthy, with a cordial invitation to consider the claims of Swarthmore College to their liberal contributions and bequests, the writer of this would close his appeal by asking those who, like himself, are still struggling toward a competence, to identify themselves with a movement promising such permanent benefits to the children of the present and future generations. Of the money thus far subscribed, much the largest part has come in subscriptions of less than one hundred dollars. The managers look for a *general duplication of these subscriptions*, and ask that every individual interested in the perpetuity of the Society of Friends, and in the welfare of the children growing up under its influence, shall become a stockholder in Swarthmore College—the rich contributing from their abundance—those in moderate circumstances in less amount—all according to their means—to establish what we confidently believe will be a great and obvious blessing for ages to come.

An association embracing the young and old, the farmer and citizen, the rich and those in moderate circumstances, the progressive and conservative, interesting all in an institution of real utility and practical advantage, must of itself, have an important influence in consolidating and perpetuating the Society in whose interest it was organized, and creating and diffusing a wholesome public spirit among its members.

KITCHEN
DINING R
W.C.
W.C
CLASS
CLASS
CORRIDOR
CLASS
CLASS
P
D
PARLOR
OFFICE
P
92
44
100
60
100
44

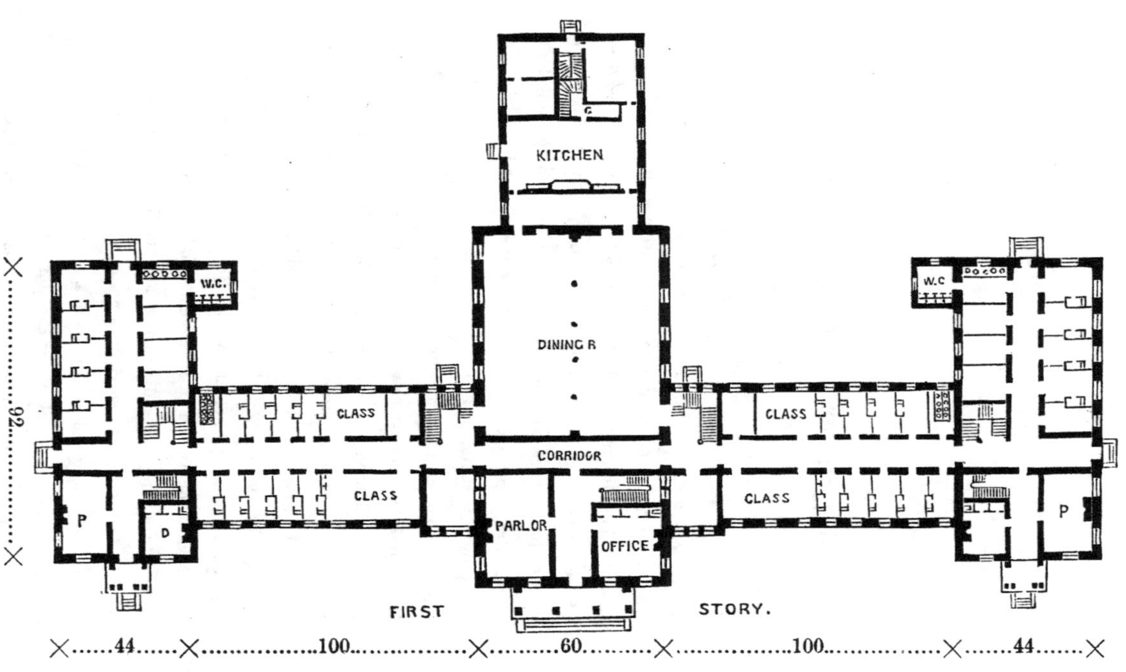

FIRST STORY.

DESCRIPTION OF THE GROUND PLAN.

First Story.—The center building will be 60 feet front by 110 feet 6 inches deep, divided, in front of the corridor which runs from end to end of the entire building, into a hall, parlor or library, office and stairway. The dining-room, in the rear of the corridor, which is 55 by 62 feet, has a carving-room attached, which, with the kitchen, is in a two-storied back building, 40 by 50 feet, containing also closet and pantries, a private dining-room for the domestics, and stairs leading to their chambers above.

On either side of the center building is a fire-proof alcove, 15 feet wide, containing iron stairways in the rear, and adapted to secure light and ventllation to the adjoining parts of the building, while it cuts off the connection between the center building and wings in case of fire. The wings, extending on either side, are each 100 feet long, including the alcoves, by 44 feet wide. On the first story they contain 4 class-rooms and 2 cloak-rooms adjoining the alcoves and stairways, 2 wash-rooms, and 18 chambers, each 10 by 15 feet.

The return wings, extending north and south, 44 by 92 feet, each contains, in front of the corridor, a parlor and living room, and private stairway, designed for the use of a resident professor or matron with their families; back of the corridor are commodious stairways, and 16 chambers, 10 by 15 feet. The water towers, marked W C, are built on a line with the rear wall adjoining the wash-rooms; they are 11 feet square in the clear.

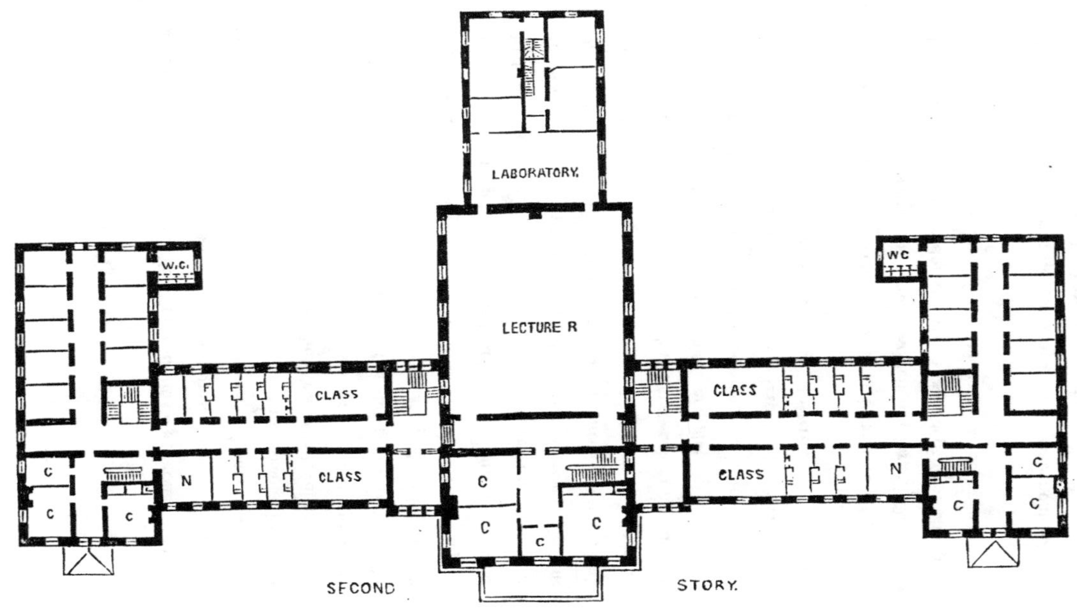

SECOND STORY.

DESCRIPTION OF THE GROUND PLAN.

Second Story.—The center building contains 4 apartments, marked C, which may be appropriated as class-rooms, lyceum-room, offices, cabinets, etc., as may be required. In the rear of this is the lecture and collecting room, of the same size as the dining-room, but with a ceiling 30 feet high, and a gallery reached from the level of the third story; a laboratory and apparatus rooms communicate with this; while the sleeping accommodations, for the domestics, which adjoin them, are reached exclusively by the private stairs from below. The arrangement of the wings in the second story is nearly the same as in the first, omitting cloak-rooms and adding two nurseries, marked N, which communicate with the private apartments, marked C, belonging to the resident professors or matrons. Nurseries designed for any cases of contagious disease which may need complete isolation, are provided in the front attics, which are commodious and thoroughly ventilated. Some of the chambers, each of which is designed to accommodate two students, have complete closets, superseding the necessity of bureau and wardrobe. In others these articles of furniture may be preferred. It is impossible to exhibit all the details of arrangement in a drawing of this size.

Third Story and Attics.—The third story is appropriated exclusively to sleeping apartments, some of which are large. The attics, which are high and contain dormer-windows, except upon the front, will furnish trunk-rooms, and, if needed, extra sleeping accommodations.

The building, as thus projected, will accommodate about 225 pupils, with the necessary teachers and attendants.

Descriptions more in detail are printed in the form of specifications.

PROCEEDINGS

ON THE

Occasion of Laying the Corner-Stone

OF

SWARTHMORE COLLEGE,

ON THE

10TH OF FIFTH MONTH, 1866.

PUBLISHED BY DIRECTION OF THE BOARD OF MANAGERS OF THE CORPORATION.

The Opening.

ON fifth day, afternoon, the tenth of fifth month, 1866, under a clear sky, and surrounded by a genial atmosphere, a company assembled on the grounds of Swarthmore College to commemorate the laying of the corner-stone of the structure about to be erected. Of those thus collected some were from New York and its vicinity, some from New Jersey, a few from Baltimore, and many from Philadelphia and the surrounding country, especially the counties of Delaware and

Chester. On a commodious platform erected at the easternmost corner of the foundations of the center building, the company were seated, or standing in groups, when the meeting was called to order by Samuel Willets, of New York, who had been selected to preside.

Letters Received.

Edward Parrish, President of the College, produced several letters received by him from individuals invited to be present, among whom were Mary S. Lippincott and Sarah Hunt, Moorestown, New Jersey; Dr. Thomas H. Kirkbride, of the Pennsylvania Hospital for the Insane; Samuel M. Janney, of Loudon County, Virginia; and Edward H. Magill, of the Boston Public Latin School, all expressive of regret at the necessity of being absent.* Portions of these were read, and the following are selected for publication :

* A letter has been since received from J. P. Wickersham, Principal of the State Normal School at Millersville, Pennsylvania, and President of the American Teacher's Association,

FROM SAMUEL M. JANNEY, *dated Lincoln, Va., 5th Mo.* 6, 1866.

EDWARD PARRISH,
PRESIDENT OF SWARTHMORE COLLEGE.

MY DEAR FRIEND:

Last evening I received thy kind letter, with a card of invitation to attend the laying of the corner-stone of the College edifice.

I regret that I cannot be present on that interesting occasion; but my heart is with you in the cause of education, which the College is intended to promote. I trust that the institution will be founded on the immutable principles of truth and love, and that it will be a blessing to the youth of our Society, and others who may share its benefits, not only in our day, but in future generations.

The improvement of the talents conferred by a bountiful Creator is a duty incumbent upon all, and in rearing the superstructure of knowledge each generation must avail itself of the labors and discoveries of its predecessors. When we look over our widely extended country and behold the products of art and industry in the form of cities and cultivated farms, in manufactures, railroads, canals, and telegraphs, we are impressed with the vast amount of accumulated wealth; but we should bear in mind that the treasures of literature and science are far more valuable and enduring, for in these are contained the elements of all improvement in the arts that minister to individual comfort or national greatness.

---

regretting his unexpected absence, which arose from circumstances beyond his control. Also one from Professor Thomas Chase, of Haverford College, who, through an accident, did not receive an invitation to attend until too late, but expresses cordial good wishes for the success of the enterprise, and desires that the cause of sound education may be promoted by it.

In view of these magnificent results, we are ready to exclaim, in the language of the poet,—

> "What cannot art and industry perform
> When science plans the progress of their toil."

It is the purpose of our higher schools and colleges to place within the reach of the student the stores of knowledge accumulated by the wise and good of former ages, and to assist in developing the intellectual powers and moral principles. In executing this great trust, the teacher of youth should ever remember that the development of the intellect, though highly important, is of far less value than the cultivation of moral excellence, and that the benign principles of Christianity can alone secure happiness here and prepare the soul for eternal felicity hereafter.

With sincere desires for the success of the institution,

I remain thy cordial friend,

SAMUEL M. JANNEY.

FROM EDWARD H. MAGILL, *dated Boston, 5th Mo.* 3, 1866.

DEAR FRIEND EDWARD PARRISH:

Thy kind letter, inviting me to be present at the laying of the corner-stone of Swarthmore, was received a few days since, and I embrace my earliest opportunity to express my deep regret that my duties here absolutely forbid me to think of being with you on that very interesting occasion. It would be an event to look back upon with great satisfaction all my life long if I could enjoy the privilege of taking part in these ceremonies, which are to constitute the first public step in one of the greatest educational works yet undertaken, I will not say by Friends alone, but in this country. Is that too much to say? If it seems extravagant now, the results, in time to come, will prove the reasonableness of my words to-day. I see in this work the inception of a movement which is to prove, what has never yet been fully proven, although tried to some extent, that it is feasible and desirable to give to woman equal educational facilities with man, not in the earlier stages of education merely, but to carry them together, *pari passu*, to the heights of literature and science, and to prepare them alike to use to the best advantage, to themselves and the world, the talents with which they are endowed. How appropriate that the movement should take place among Friends, who recognize more fully than others the equality of the sexes, and among whom it is not considered "a shame for a woman to speak in the church." When I reflect upon the great advance in public sentiment in this regard during the present century, that here in Boston, which claims, justly or unjustly, to be the fountain-head of progress in educational, as in other matters, it was not deemed necessary to give girls the benefit of public school instruction till 1780, that from 1780 until 1820 they were allowed to occupy in the grammar schools the vacant seats of the boys in summer only, and that until 1852 no high school for girls was established here, except one which lived for but two years, but which was suppressed as an unnecessary expenditure of the public money by the efforts of Mayor Quincy; when I reflect, I say, upon these changes, I can but feel encouraged to hope that another half century will see every college in our country accessible to both sexes alike. I say a half century, that I may be wholly within the limit of probability; I wish I could reasonably say less, but I know too well the conservative tendency of old-established literary institutions. As creeds are but dead beliefs, named, numbered, and labeled, so it is too true of our great universities, that they are the sacred depositaries of the ideas of former generations instead of organized bodies of learned men adapting themselves readily to the progress of the race. The result of this mingling of the sexes upon the scholarship of our colleges cannot be prejudicial, and I feel confident that it will have an opposite effect; while the influence of such a change upon the morals and manners of the young men must be highly advantageous. In this great work of popularizing education, in the truest sense of that word, I trust Swarthmore is destined to take the lead.

I regret to learn that some Friends who have the means to place this College at once upon a firm foundation are lukewarm and inactive in this movement. Do they not see that the time has fully come when such an institution among Friends is demanded by the advancing spirit of the age? Would they see the best minds in the Society gradually alienated from it by seeking outside of its limits that culture which they cannot obtain within its fold? Do they not know that it is inevitable, if young Friends obtain their education among others, that they should very frequently become estranged from the principles and practices of the Society, and attach themselves to other religious organizations? Such has been the case in the past, to a greater or less extent, and it must be increasingly so in the future, as the demand increases for that culture which Friends are not in a condition to give. How many there are with growing families who would gladly keep their children wholly under the influence of Friends, but who wish to give them a more comprehensive education and a more liberal culture than can at present be obtained in the Society!

A graduate of Harvard recently died in Boston at an advanced age, leaving a large estate to be divided among his children. Among other bequests was one of $5000 to his *Alma Mater*. This having been mentioned as an act of generosity worthy of imitation, a writer in one of our dailies has recently shown very clearly that it was scarcely more than simple *honesty*, for it was but the partial payment of a debt which was justly due to an institution which, at a trifling expense to himself, gave him that for which money could be no adequate return, and by four years of careful training, laid the sure foundation for his future career of success and usefulness in this community. One of his sons, at least, has since acknowledged the justice of the claim by adding $20,000 to the benefaction of his father.

Cannot those Friends who are blessed with an abundance of this world's goods be made to feel that, if they value the Society of their fathers, and esteem it a privilege above all price that their lot has been cast where they could enjoy the communion of kindred spirits in that Society, it is a sacred duty which they owe to the rising generation to see that ample and sure provision is made for the continuance of this privilege unimpaired to them during the period devoted to acquiring an education?

I need scarcely remind you, as you are laying the corner-stone of the College building, that, noble as will be the structure of stone and brick and mortar piled upon it, it is not the building which the College occupies that is to give it character, as compared with other institutions of learning. If, as you lay the solid granite of its corner-stone, you firmly resolve that you—its founders—will never rest satisfied, or feel that your work is accomplished, while, in respect to the organization, to the arrangement of the course of study, or to aught that goes to make up the *real* and not the merely *material* college, anything remains undone which untiring energy and perseverance on your part can accomplish, then indeed will this significant act be no useless form.

Let us hope that in the future Swarthmore College will not be allowed to turn aside from the course marked out for it, thus early, by its far-sighted and beneficent originators, as an institution for general and liberal culture, and become a mere practical school, so called, for the preparation for the special duties of life. It must not be allowed to make one-sided men and women, cultivating only such faculties as are already, perhaps, too prominent, and need repression instead of cultivation; but its course of studies should be so arranged as to provide a broad and generous culture for all, whatever their career in life may be destined to be. The most zealous advocates for a "limited education" admit that the preliminary course of instruction should be the same for all. Of course, the question arises, where this general preliminary education should end and special education commence? I trust that in this regard we do not intend to imitate, in the new College, the example of those who ignore whatever does not bear very directly upon the practical duties of life. That special training for a particular occupation or profession is essential, we certainly all admit; but do not let us encourage the strong bias of the present generation toward materialistic views by admitting, either by word or deed, that education is valuable only as it tends, directly or indirectly, toward the production of creature comforts, the accumulation of wealth, or the promotion of our individual or national outward prosperity.

Deeply impressed with these views, and resting my belief in their ultimate realization upon the fact that Friends aim to be a peculiarly spiritually-minded people, I anticipate a bright future for Swarthmore, confidently believing that some of us will live to see the day when our new College will compare favorably with the best in the land, nobly pursuing an independent course, yet not disdaining to imitate the excellences of all, while scrupulously avoiding their defects and errors.

Very truly, thy friend,

E. H. MAGILL.

After the reading of the letters, the following address was read by the President of the College:

Address of Edward Parrish.

About five years and a half have passed since the inception of the project which has taken form in Swarthmore College; about two, since we became possessed of this beautiful site: and now we meet to take the first formal step toward the erection of the edifice which is to embody our well-considered plans of building. We begin the erection on this elevated plateau of a stone structure 348 feet long, consisting of a center building 60 by 138 feet, and two return wings 44 by 92 feet, connected by intermediate wings 44 by 100 feet. The whole will be three stories high, and the center building will be surmounted by an observatory, from which the eye will take in an extended panorama of Delaware County, with its fertile farms, busy mills, and peaceful villages, while the Counties of Gloucester and Camden, in New Jersey, will skirt the horizon on the east, with the broad Delaware and its shipping intervening.

With a view to make this building worthy of the site and the noble object to which it is to be appropriated, it is designed to be complete in all its arrangements for the accommodation of the extensive family of inmates and for the illustration of all the branches of knowledge in which they are to be instructed.

The most substantial materials will be used in its construction, the extensive corridors being of brick work to the roof, which will be of slate, and the five sections of the building being separated by solid fireproof divisions, the whole will constitute a remarkably enduring monument to the far-seeing liberality of its founders.

In accordance with a time-honored custom, we propose to deposit in this most eastern corner of the center building a corner-stone, containing a receptacle, to be tightly inclosed, in which we shall place fitting memorials of the times in which we live, to the end that when, centuries hence, these massive walls shall be demolished or rebuilt, the antiquarian who with eager curiosity shall explore our work, shall find something to add to that chain of facts by which men instinctively love to trace the progress of the ages. Before these walls shall have crumbled, every one of us, with our plans of domestic enjoyment and of personal aggrandizement, all our family and social interests and concernments, will be forgotten. The absorbing political questions which now so tax the mind of the nation will then have been solved by the lapse of time. No one living can predict, except with the eye of faith, that future which shall become the present before the tokens which we now deposit are removed.

It may teach us a lesson of humility to think that even our sectarian theories and prejudices—the faiths many and the forms many about which men contend and with which they build up partitions in society—are transient, even when compared with the stones and mortar which the stalwart mason cements into his solid walls.

Many of the set phrases in which the theologian would confine the universal truths of God will cease to have their present conventional meaning, — some of our most cherished words will become obsolete,—the finest passages in our literature will sound quaint to those who in some far distant time will exhume this corner-stone, and with curious interest seek to lay open its mysteries.

Let none accuse us of personal vanity in depositing our photographs and autographs in this box; the comments they may elicit from those who next will look upon them will be harmless to excite our vanity or to wound our self-love; and in transmitting to posterity the lineaments of some who have shared in this work, we do but gratify in our successors what we all recognize as a harmless curiosity in ourselves.

This occasion marks another step toward the organization of Swarthmore College, with a full corps of professors and teachers, and complete facilities for imparting sound and liberal learning, and it may be thought appropriate that a concise statement should be given of the educational views which have influenced its originators.

Called by the unanimous choice of the Managers, and without my own solicitation, to preside over its organization, I bring to the work one leading qualification of which I am conscious: a thorough conviction of the utility, not to say necessity, of the establishment of our college, coupled with a high ideal of what such an institution ought to be.

That the result will fall short of this ideal is of course inevitable, but our ideal is not the less valuable that we cannot expect in our time to realize its complete attainment.

1. We aim to educate the sexes together, each wing of our building will be separately allotted to one or the other, the collecting-room, dining-room, library and class-rooms are for their joint occupancy. The grounds will doubtless be in some degree divided and appropriated for their separate use, while in many sports they will participate together.

Impressed with the great loss resulting to society from estranging young men and women from each other during the years that are especially devoted to moral and intellectual development, we mean to seek after and follow the natural law of social and domestic intercourse, and to strip their converse as far as possible of any glowing halo of romance, to clothe it with an investment of friendship and good sense.

2. We shall propose a high grade of intellectual attainment for those who seek our diploma. The idea incorporated into the first draft of our plan was that of an institution in which an education could be obtained equal to that furnished by the best colleges in the land. While it is obvious that this standard can only be attained as the result of maturity in the institution, yet this high aim is essential to be kept in view from the very start.

An Academical department will necessarily precede the opening of the college classes, and will probably be a permanent feature of the institution. The standard of admission to this will be advanced as opportunity allows, and all the studies will be adapted to prepare the students for the collegiate course.

Instruction in the art of teaching will be a desideratum, and in the future a model school will probably be opened to facilitate this important practical branch.

3. The relative importance to be attached in our College to the three main departments of Mathematics, Language, and Science has already been somewhat discussed among those interested in its establishment.

While these considerations can only be fully determined when the faculty shall be organized, it has been generally understood among us that the study of those branches of science pertaining to the physical universe, which have been so rapidly advanced by modern investigations, and are so wonderfully adapted to develop the intellect and to increase our appreciation of the wisdom and goodness of the Creator, will here have a place not yet conceded to them in colleges established before they had reached their present magnitude and importance.

Yet I trust none of us will be disposed to undervalue those abstract studies which are so remarkably adapted to train the reasoning powers, nor language, the study of which, as a means of mental discipline, has been so long esteemed, and the importance of which, as an aid to the appreciation and expression of great truths, none will dispute.

It is a false idea of education which limits it to any one class of studies or degrades it to a mere utilitarian basis. Nothing is deserving the name which does not enlarge man's nature and fit him for the enjoyment of elevating thoughts and ideas out of the range of business. And yet there is no honorable pursuit in life for which a man is not better fitted by that accumulation of knowledge, that power of classifying facts and ideas and of deducing principles from them, which it is the object of a liberal education to impart.

We claim a higher mission for Swarthmore College than that of fitting men and women for business—it should fit them for life, with all its possibilities. May those who shall hereafter guide its destinies be inspired with a love of learning for its own sake, and for the inestimable advantages it is capable of conferring, and may they never cease to couple in their system of training the highest intellectual culture with the development of the moral and religious elements of character.

4. The leading motive of those who have originated this movement has been what in the familiar phrase of Friends is called a *guarded* education. It is our desire to give its proper place to that feature of moral training

—almost distinctive of the Society of Friends—which rests upon a recognition of the intuitive sense of right and wrong implanted by the Creator in every rational soul. This, recognized in its full force, supersedes much of the religious instruction which is considered essential in most of the Christian churches. With it, the precepts of Christianity become vital and saving. Without it, they are liable to lead into formality,—into a verbal and ceremonial faith.

It is impossible to exaggerate the importance of education in its connection with the moral attributes of our nature—born on the confines of two boundless worlds, a world of infinite joy and a world of immeasurable sorrow, obligations reaching through all eternity attach themselves to the human soul from very infancy.

Great is the responsibility of the parent who essays to guide the infant mind in its first efforts to exercise that free agency which is the high prerogative of its nature, and scarcely less, that of the teacher who is to pilot the intellect as it sets sail into the vast ocean of conflicting thoughts and opinions. Let both see to it that through no fault of theirs a cloud shall obscure "that light which lighteth every man that cometh into the world." "For," says the wise man, "the commandment is a lamp, and the law is light, and the reproofs of instruction are the way of life."

Let me remind our fellow-citizens not of the Society of Friends, who from interest in the cause of education or from motives of a personal or local character, have given us their presence to-day, that although the Society has long been identified with certain testimonies which have led many of its members into peculiarities by which they are known in the community, it is in no offensive sense sectarian; nor are Friends propagandists.

The founders of the Society were among the foremost advocates of the most enlarged civil and religious liberty, not for themselves only, but for all; and while they have sometimes advocated their views with considerable zeal, they have not aimed to proselyte to their own peculiar forms and organization.

Content to spread their principles among all religious sects and civil communities, they have witnessed their partial incorporation into the prevailing sentiment of most Protestant communities, and their introduction into the civil polity of almost every State in this vast Union of Commonwealths.

Is it not cause of general congratulation that here in Delaware County, within sight of the first landing-place of William Penn in his Province, his successors in religious communion should erect a capacious and permanent institution in which the principles and even the forms to which he was conscientiously bound, and for which he sacrificed so much of worldly preferment, will obtain favorable consideration and encouragement?

An institution in which the glorious testimony to a free gospel ministry, exercised equally by men and women without the necessity of special education, shall be held up before the youth whose characters are forming under the influence of teachers of talent and learning. In which the inconsistency of war with pure Christianity shall be made a matter of careful and conscientious examination, to the end that the promised day may be hastened when "nation shall not lift up a sword against nation, neither shall they learn war any more." In which truth and duty shall be set far above expediency, and obedience to law be taught as limited only by the paramount obligations of conscience. In which the Christian democracy of early Friends shall be so far maintained as to abolish within its domain all precedence founded on birth or riches, bringing all under the equalizing and elevating influence of intelligence and culture.

As Pennsylvanians, we may well hold up to our children the early history of this Commonwealth as an illustration of the predominance of moral over physical force even in conducting the affairs of a State; and as Friends, we may present to their view the example of a long line of worthy ancestors who illustrated, by consistent lives, the power of pure morality and Christian principle.

Our efforts to establish and maintain Swarthmore College can only be successful by the blessing of Divine Providence; and in proportion as those selected to conduct it seek and obtain this blessing, the College will diffuse an influence for good, not to those alone who may participate directly in its benefits, but to the whole Society of Friends and the community at large.

Laying of the Corner-Stone.

At the close of this address, a metallic box was produced, into which were introduced the following articles:

Silver and copper coins, fractional currency, and postage stamps, of the current year.

Newspapers of Philadelphia and New York, and of Delaware County, Pennsylvania, Friends' Intelligencer and Friends' Review, and The Children's Friend, West Chester, Pennsylvania.

Relics of Swarthmore Hall and Meeting-House, near Ulverstone, England, contributed by Samuel Smedley.

"Address of Some Members of the Religious Society of Friends to their Fellow Members on Education," issued in 1860; "Education in the Society of Friends, Past, Present, and Prospective, by Edward Parrish," 1865; Annual Reports and other papers issued by the Managers of Swarthmore College.

Subscription papers of 1861 and 1866, proof impression of the corporate seal, and a certificate of stock.

Photographs of original and present plans of the prospective buildings, photographs of the Architects, and of the Managers of the College, and numerous other Friends, countersigned with their respective autographs;

9*

also a few additional mementoes contributed by those present.

The box was then tightly soldered up and deposited by the Chairman in the corner-stone, in which an excavation had been made to receive it.

The corner-stone was then laid in its place in a bed of mortar by George Diemer, the contractor for the masonry of the building.

After the company had resumed their seats, Dr. J. Thomas, of Philadelphia, was introduced, and addressed those assembled as follows:

Remarks of Dr. Joseph Thomas.

In the very brief remarks which I propose to offer on the present occasion, I wish it to be understood that I am an "outsider," and consequently, though I feel a deep interest in the object which has brought us together, the originators of this great enterprise are in nowise responsible for anything that I may happen to say.

I need scarcely observe that I am far from desiring in any way to strengthen the barriers which divide the various denominations of Christians, yet so long as there are different sects, I rejoice that all are to be represented in the great cause of liberal education.

It is doubtless a good and glorious thing for our country, that we have everywhere elementary schools in which all, even the humblest, may acquire the rudiments of an English education; but what would society be if we had nothing higher than these?

In my opinion, what we Americans have most to fear, is a dead level of mediocrity in the education of our people. In the economy of nature it is important that some portions of the earth's surface should be more elevated than the rest; for a country wholly destitute of mountains or hills can have in itself neither fertility nor beauty—all the fertility of Egypt is derived through the Nile from the mountains of central Africa—and I believe the influence of a superior class of educated men serves to give life and spirit, and efficiency to the knowledge of the masses.

Many persons seem to suppose that a moderate education, if joined with good common sense, is sufficient for all the purposes of life. It may be all that is needed for ordinary occasions, but not for the higher objects of our existence.

It is undeniably true, that while education in the United States is perhaps more generally diffused than in any other part of the world, there are in proportion to the whole number of our people fewer thoroughly educated men than, I will not say in any other country in Christendom, but certainly fewer than in any of the more enlightened countries of Europe, including, I might say, France and all the Protestant nations. Hence it has sometimes happened that works professedly of a learned or scientific character, but of the merest pretension, have met with great favor even among the most intelligent of our people. A single example may suffice. The principal doctrines of "Nott and Gliddon's Types of Mankind" were a few years ago accepted as undoubted truth by many of our most intelligent citizens and scientific men, and indeed were so accepted by the editor of *Putnam's Magazine*, one of the most respectable critical journals published in the United States; but I think no instance can be presented of a single scientific man or scientific journal of any standing in Europe having been taken in by the shallow learning and loose science of the work above named.

I trust I shall not be understood as seeking to disparage my country, for I am very proud of her,—I admit that she excels in many things; what I desire is that she should excel in everything.

We ought, I think, to be especially on our guard, that we be not deceived by the cry of utility which we hear on every hand. True, in its largest sense, the useful may include all that is most desirable for the human race, but it is too often limited to merely providing for our physical wants and necessities. In this sense it excludes the love of the beautiful and the cultivation of all those sentiments which constitute the chief glory of man. Such views if carried out would paralyze or destroy all that is noblest and most beautiful in the human character; they would in fact reduce the race of man to the condition of two-legged beavers—animals ingenious, sagacious, industrious, but nothing more. Happily the Creator has given us instincts that render it impossible for any people to carry such a system of utilitarianism to its ultimate results, but it may easily be carried much farther than would be consistent with the highest interest or happiness of mankind.

Those who pursue science and truth for their own sake, really do far more to promote the useful in the best sense of the word than those whose sole object begins and ends with utility. Does any one suppose that Sir Isaac Newton was influenced by mere considerations of utility when he made his immortal discovery of the laws which govern the universe?

I am one of those who believe that the importance of education in its truest and highest sense has never yet been overestimated.

We should, my friends, I am convinced, commit a great mistake were we to suppose that the influence of such an institution as we are founding to-day will be limited to those only or chiefly who shall be educated within its halls. On the contrary, it will extend to the whole community—to the entire country. The founding of such an institution is indeed a distinct and emphatic annunciation to the world of our belief in the great importance of a high and liberal culture. It is a declaration of eternal war against the realms of ignorance and darkness; it is a proclamation to all mankind that we for our part have faith in light and science and truth, and do not fear to follow them whithersoever they may lead us.

In concluding, I would say that, although an alumnus of next to the oldest college in the United States, I do not on that account the less sincerely or less cordially wish a God-speed to this young institution, whose existence may be said to date from to-day. May its success be complete; may its career be long and glorious; may it prove to be a true and faithful foster-mother to those committed to its care; and may it be instrumental in diffusing among its children and others the light, not only of true learning and science, but, what is of far higher importance, of moral and religious truth.

Treasurer's Statement.

William Canby Biddle, Treasurer of the Corporation, followed upon the pecuniary aspects of the enterprise, inviting a liberal response to the call for additional funds which would necessarily be made before the work could be complete.

Besides the subscriptions previously made, amounting to about $65,000, in sums varying from $25 to $1000, a special subscription has been started, during the past year, of sums of $1000 and upwards, now reaching $35,000, designed to reach an aggregate of $100,000. If this can be accomplished, through the liberality of those blessed with large means, and a general duplication made of the original subscriptions and new subscriptions obtained from all interested, according to their means, a sum will be realized which will enable the Managers to complete the buildings now commenced, and to furnish and equip them with every facility for the objects in view.

Although this occasion was not deemed appropriate to enlarge upon this subject, it was thought due to some now present at one of our meetings for the first time, that a statement should be made of the financial condition and prospects of the concern.

The Close.

The importance of this occasion, as inaugurating a work of such magnitude, and the feeling that it can only prosper through the favor of Omnipotence, led the company assembled to appropriate a few moments to solemn silence, during which, though no voice was raised, many hearts were drawn into earnest prayer that the Divine blessing may rest upon Swarthmore College, not only during its incipient stages, but throughout all the future that may be before it.

www.ingramcontent.com/pod-product-compliance
Lightning Source LLC
LaVergne TN
LVHW021430110826
845150LV00007B/2165

9781425506544